CRICKET
A MOM'S GUIDE TO HER KIDS' FAVORITE SPORT

BY

MIRIAM RICE-WALCOTT

Indoor Nets photo courtesy of
The Gentlemen of West London Cricket Club
Cricket Scoring Guide by cricket.or.jp/wp-content

www.bluepalmpublications.com

ISBN: 13: 978-1722164010
ISBN: 10: 1722164018

This book is also available as an eBook and as a downloadable PDF from www.bluepalmpublications.com

We respect your feedback and would appreciate it if you can leave a review to inform future buyers.

ABOUT THIS BOOK

As the game of cricket grows in popularity in countries like North America, many moms are find that they are on the side of cricket fields, happy to support their kids in this activity, but not understanding what they are watching. Cricket - A moms guide to her kids' favorite sport will elevate you to rock star status when you can communicate your understanding of the game with them. From "appeals" to "Yorkers" you'll soon be speaking the same language.

Inside this handy travel size book you will find a brief history of the development of the game, synopsis of the major variations of the game and the major terms used in the game, with some of their origins and meanings. The main feature of this handy book is an extensive glossary/index for easy reference. There is also an illustrated guide to umpire signals and a guide on how to score with scoring sheets that can be printed out and used. Full colour pictures as illustration to some of the text appear throughout this book.

This book is also available on Kindle where the Glossary has active links making it easy to navigate from one section to another on phone or tablet as you sit on the sidelines.

This book is not an encyclopedia of the game nor is it a rule book.. Where it does refer to rules hey are up to date as to the last ICC (International Cricket Council) update in 2018.

Cricket - A mom's guide to her kids favorite sport will leave you with an understanding of this enjoyable game beloved by many people around the world.

TABLE OF CONTENTS

AN OVERVIEW OF THE GAME

The professional game of cricket is played on a large ground with two teams made up of eleven on field players and one substitute known as the "twelfth man". There are two on field Umpires, two sets of stumps complete with bails. A bat and a ball. The object of the game for the batting side is to make as many runs as they can off the balls being bowled at them by the opposing team. The object of the game for the fielding side is to get each batsman from the batting side out as quickly as possible, conceding as few runs as possible. The Umpires are there to ensure that there is fair play and that the rules of the game are followed.

To start a match the opposing Captains take part in a coin toss. The home teams' Captain will toss the coin while the visiting Captain will make the call of heads or tails before the coin hits the ground. The captain winning the toss takes into consideration the playing conditions and the strength and weaknesses of his own players and those of the opposing team before deciding whether to bat first or send in the opposing team to take first 'knock'.

The Umpires walk on to the ground where they take up positions, one at the bowlers end and the other at square leg. They are closely followed by the eleven players of the fielding side who take up their positions around the field. All eleven remain on the field throughout the batting teams' innings. The two opening batsmen of the opposing team take up their positions at the crease. These batsmen are expected to lay a solid foundation for the other team members to follow. The "middle order" is made up of competent batsmen who can build on the foundation. The "tailenders" are lesser batsmen usually made up of the specialist bowlers of the side. Their batting prowess is not always to be under estimated as many a Test Match has come to a nail biting finish as the result of the batsmanship of a team's "tailenders".

The bowler sets his mark, the batsman takes guard, the bowler's end umpire consults his watch, the other on field umpire, the official scorers, the fielding Captain and the batsmen at the crease. When all are ready the umpire calls "play", and the game begins.

Please note that the game of Cricket is played by both males and females. Where ever the term "he" may be used throughout this book, unless otherwise stated, it applies to both male and female players equally.

GLOSSARY

ALL OUT

When ten of the eleven members of the team have been dismissed. (see page 16 Dismissals)

ALL ROUNDER

A player who is capable of batting, bowling and fielding competently. The most famous player to fall into this category is Sir Garfield Sobers of Barbados and the West Indies. In Tests, as a batsman he scored 8032 runs at an average of 57.78. As a bowler Sobers took 235 wickets with a best of 6-73 at an average of 34.03, with a best of 6 for 73. In the field he took 109 catches. He held the record for the most runs scored in a Test Match, 365 not out (a record which stood for 36 years until Brian Lara of Trinidad & Tobago and the West Indies scored 375 in 1994).

APPEAL

A loud call made to the Umpire for a batsman to be given out. "How's that?" (sounding more like "Howzatt")is the usual call. It should be noted that while some dismissals are clear cut, Law 27 states that in certain circumstances an Umpire cannot give a batsman out unless there is an Appeal from a member of the fielding side.

AVERAGES

1. **BATSMAN'S AVERAGE** =

Number of runs scored

Number of Innings batted
Minus The number of times not out

2. **BOWLER'S AVERAGE** =

Number of runs conceded

Number of wickets taken

BAILS

Two wooden cross pieces over the top of the Stumps. Each bail measures 4.31" (10.95cm).

Two Wooden Bails Sitting Atop Three Stumps

BALL

In the First Class game and Test Cricket the ball used is round and encased in stitched leather. It can be up to 9 inches

(22.9 cm) in circumference but not less than 8.81 inches (22.4 cm). It's weight should be no less than 5.5 ounces (155 g) and no more than 5.75 ounces (163 g). This applies to the male version of the game. The dimensions for Female Cricket are 4.94 ounces (140g) to 5.31ounces and (151g) 8.25" (21.0cm) to 8.8" (22.5cm).

In the One Day game and night cricket the ball used is white or pink in colour.

A Cricket Ball Showing the Raised Seams

BAT

Bats are traditionally made from English Willow with cane handles and should not be longer than 38 inches (96.52cm) or wider than 4.25 inches.(10.8cm) Depth: 2.64inches (6.7 cm) Edges: 1.56inches (4.0cm).

The flat front part of the bat is known as the blade and this is the part the batsman uses to hit the ball with.

In 1979 the Australian cricketer Dennis Lillee walked on to the field of play with an aluminum bat. It was not well received.

BATSMAN/BATTER

All the members of the team are expected to bat in the match. However the first five batsmen in a team are considered to be the specialist batsmen.

BOUNCER

A fast Short Pitched delivery which reaches the batsman at shoulder height or above.

BOUNDARY

1. The inner edge of the perimeter of the playing field which should be clearly marked with a rope, drawn line, fence, or other type of marker.

2. When the ball crosses or touches a boundary marker, the batsman is said to have "struck a boundary".

BOWLED

A form of Dismissal. For a batsman to be bowled the ball bowled at him must hit the wicket and dislodge a bail.

A Batsman Clean Bowled

The ball can hit the wicket directly or come off the batsman's bat or person.

BOWLER

Each team will have four or five specialist bowlers. They are either Fast Bowlers, Spin Bowlers or variations of either.

BYES

Any runs made when the ball passes the wicket untouched by the bat or body of the batsman (See page 23 leg byes).

CAP

Team headwear presented to a player on his debut match. Players may accumulate a series of Caps from each Test that they play. The Australian Cap is nicknamed the "Baggy Green" and was first worn around the turn of the 20th Century.

CARRY THE BAT

An opening batsman who is not out at the end of an innings either at the end of a day's play or a match. is said to have "carried his bat".

CAUGHT

Another form of dismissal. A batsman is out caught if he hits the ball with the bat, glove or hand holding the bat and it is caught by a fielder within the playing area before it hits the ground.

CENTURY

A hundred runs scored by an individual batsman.

Ellis Achong

CHINAMAN

The left arm bowlers off break to a right handed batsman. Legend has it that the term got its name from Ellis Achong, a Trinidadian of Chinese descent who played for the West Indies. It was his unorthodox delivery getting an English batsman out that is said to have prompted the remark that he was "done in by a Chinaman".

CLEAN BOWLED

When a delivery hits the stumps and removes the bails without being touched by the batsman.

COVERS

1. The equipment used to cover the pitch to protect the surface, usually from rain.

2. The fielding position between Point and Mid Off. (See Page 53 Fielding Positions)

CREASE

There are 3 sets of creases marked with painted lines at each end of the pitch.

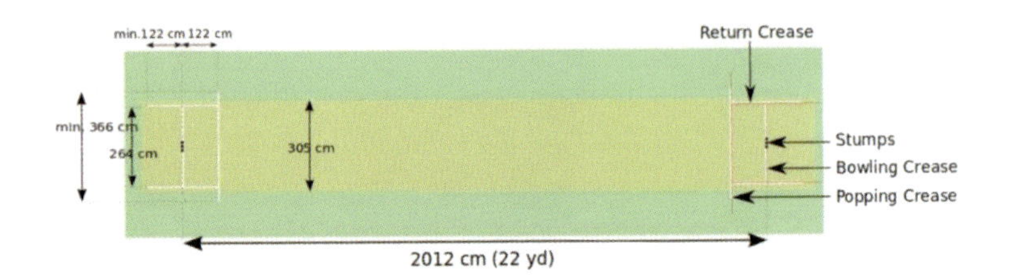

Diagram Showing the Layout of the Pitch & Creases

1. The **Bowling Crease** is the line along which the stumps are set.
2. The **Popping Crease** is positioned parallel to the bowling crease with four feet between them.
3. The **Return Crease** is at right angles from each end of the bowling creases extending past the popping crease (See diagram above)

DECLARATION

The Captain of the batting side can declare an innings over at any time, in matches where both teams have two innings each. The declaration is usually made in an effort to effect a result in a game rather than let the match be drawn.

DELIVERY

Each time the ball is bowled it is called a delivery. There are six deliveries in each over.

DISMISSAL

A batsman can be dismissed in one of the following ways:

1. Bowled (See page 13)
2. Caught (See page 14)
3. Hit Wicket (See page 22)
4. Hitting the Ball Twice (See page 21)
5. Leg Before Wicket (LBW) (See page 22)
6. Obstructing the Field (See page 27)
7. Run Out (See page 32)
8. Stumped (See page 36)
9. Timed Out (See page 37)

DOT BALL

The dot (period) is used instead of zero (0) by the scorer in the score book when no run comes off a bowled ball or delivery.

DRAW

Any match with two innings per side which fails to produce a result. Not to be confused with a Tie.

DUCK

When a batsman is given out without having scored any runs. Not something for any self-respecting batsman to be proud of. It is therefore not surprising that the record for the most Ducks in a Test Match career is held by a bowler, Courtney Walsh of the West Indies, who was out 43 times without scoring. He also holds the record for Diamond Ducks (being out without facing a delivery, such as being run out) and Golden Ducks (out first ball faced).

DUCKWORTH LEWIS STERN SYSTEM

A mathematical system which sets revised targets in rain interrupted limited over matches.

EXTRAS

Runs added to the batting teams' score other than by the batsman scoring. These include Byes, Leg Byes, Wides and No Balls. (See Penalty Runs Page 29)

FIELDING

There are 34 basic positions for a field set for a right handed batsman (See page 53 Fielding Positions)

FLIPPER

A leg spin delivery with under spin that bounces lower than normal. An action first accredited to the Australian spin bowler Clarrie Grimmett who played Test Cricket between 1924 and 1936 and perfected by another Australian spinner Shane Warne.

FOLLOW ON

In a match of two innings per side the team batting second can be asked to bat again if at the end of their first innings they have failed to reach the total set by the first batting side. This shortfall is determined by the number of days the game is to be played.

1. In a five day match 200 runs.

2. In a three/four day match 150 runs.
3. In a two day match 100 runs.
4. In a One Day match with two innings per side 75 runs

FREE HIT

In the limited overs version of the game a Front Foot No Ball is followed by a "free hit".

The batsman cannot be bowled or caught from this delivery but he can be Run Out.

FRONT FOOT NO BALL

A front foot no ball is incurred when a bowler over steps the popping crease whilst completing a delivery.

FULL TOSS

A ball which reaches the batsman without touching the pitch/ground. Deliberate Front Foot No Balls and Full Tosses are treated as extras.

GLOVES

Protective gloves are worn by both batsmen and the Wicket Keeper. The batsman's gloves have a leather palm for firm grip of the bat and the outside has extra padding to protect the fingers.

The Wicket Keepers gloves are all leather and leather lined with cane and sponge protectors built in.

GOOGLY

Also known as a "Wrong 'un". An Off Break bowled with a Leg Break action, that is, the ball is made to spin from off side to leg side into the right handed batsman. The bowler achieves this by rotating the wrist so that the ball rolls out of the back of the hand on delivery.

GROUND

The batsman's ground is the area between the Popping Crease and the Bowling Crease. Some part of the bat held by the batsman or part of his/her body must be on the popping, or between the two creases to be grounded. This is particularly important in run out and stumping decisions.

Also the term used for the venue of a cricket match i.e. "Lords" in England or "Kensington Oval" in Barbados.

GUARD

The batsman positions his bat in relation to the Stumps at the wicket. The Umpire at the bowlers end helps him to line up his position. The guards commonly asked for are

1. Off
2. Middle and Off,
3. Middle,
4. Middle and Leg
5. Leg.

GULLY

A fielding position close in to the pitch between the slips and point.

HALF VOLLEY

A delivery which bounces near to the front foot and is hit on the rise.

HAT TRICK

When a bowler takes three wickets with three consecutive deliveries, which can be spread over more than one over.

HAWK EYE

A computer generated program used by the Third Umpire to determine whether a ball pitched and would've hit the Stumps had the batsman not obstructed it's path. Particularly called for to confirm the on field Umpire decision in the case of LBW decisions.

HELMETS

Protective helmets are made from a carbon fiber and Kevlar material with a metal grill. Helmets are commonly worn by both batsmen and close fielders to protect against injury.

HITTING THE BALL TWICE

A rare form of Dismissal which occurs when the batsman hits the ball with his bat or person after the ball has already been played, except when trying to protect his wicket. If the ball was legitimately hit no runs can be scored.

HIT WICKET

Another form of Dismissal where the batsman dislodges the bails with his bat or any part of his person (hand, glove, cap, foot etc.). He is not out if this happens in an attempt to avoid being stumped or run out.

This is governed by Law 31:1 and was once used as a ploy by batsmen to end their innings.

INNINGS

The number of times each team bats. In a Test Match there are two innings per side. In the One Day game and T20 Cricket each team has only one innings.

KWICK CRICKET

An informal version of the game specifically designed to introduce children to the game. Plastic bats and balls are used and plastic cones mark out the area of the field which can vary depending upon the number of children playing and their age group.

LBW (LEG BEFORE WICKET)

There are a number of things that an Umpire has to take into consideration before accepting an Appeal for an LBW (leg before wicket)decision and he has only a split second in which to do so.

The most important factor to be considered is whether the ball pitched outside of leg stump and if it would have gone on to hit the Stumps.

The Umpire must also take into account the height the ball bounces, its swing and spin, whether the ball hit the pad and if the batsman was genuinely trying to play a shot.

LEG BREAK

A delivery by a right arm bowler which runs from the Leg Side towards the On Side after pitching.

LEG BYES

Where runs are made when the ball comes off the body of the batsman other than off the bat or hand holding the bat while attempting to play the ball. (See page 14 Byes)

LEG SIDE

The side of the field to the left of the receiving batsman as he takes his stance at the crease.

LEG SPIN

A form of bowling where the bowler spins the ball by turning the wrist as the ball is bowled.

The stock delivery of a leg spinner is the Leg Break. (See page 23)

LINE AND LENGTH

A term used to describe when the bowler bowls a ball which pitches just outside the off stump so that the batsman is forced to play a shot or be bowled out. The bowler is said to have bowled a good " line and length".

LONG HOP

A delivery from a bowler that is short and usually gives the batsman plenty of time to play a shot.

MAIDEN OVER

Where a bowler completes an over without any runs, no balls or wides conceded.

MAIDEN WICKET

The first wicket taken by a bowler in his career.

MARKS

A mark is used by fast bowler's to gauge the length of their run ups when bowling. It is a small round disc placed on the field

NELSON

(So named after Admiral Nelson – one eye, one arm, one leg)

A score of 111 either of a team or an individual batsman regarded by some to be unlucky because the 111 looks like the wicket without bails which happens when a batsman is out.

The superstitious custom is for each member of the batting side not on the field of play to take one foot off the ground.

NETS

Name given to the practice Pitch for both batsmen and bowlers which is surrounded on three sides by netting.

A Modern Indoor Net Facility

NEW BALL

A new ball may be taken by the Captain of the fielding side after 80 overs have been bowled in a Test Match.

In the First Class game this number may vary by competition and territory.

NIGHT WATCHMAN

The term given to a batsman who is promoted up the order towards the end of a day's play. The reasoning behind this practice is that it preserves a more valuable batsman's wicket for play the next day.

NO BALL

A delivery which an umpire considers to be unfair, often incurred by bowlers over stepping the popping crease as they complete a delivery.

The Square Leg Umpire will also call "no ball" if in his opinion the bowlers arm is bent at the point of delivery.

A single run is added to the batting team score.

The bowler is required to bowl another ball in order that the required amount of legitimate balls (6) are bowled in an over.

NON STRIKER

The batsman standing at the same end from which the bowler will make his delivery.

NOT OUT

A batsman who is in and has not been dismissed either at the end of a day's play or a match.

OBSTRUCTING THE FIELD

Where a batsman deliberately gets in the way of a fielder while fielding the ball or where a fielder deliberately gets in the way of a batsman while running between the wickets.

The contents of the former "handled ball" law has been deleted and its contents incorporated into the obstructing the field law.

OFF BREAK

An Off Spin delivery made by a right handed bowler to a right handed batsman where the ball turns from the Off Side to Leg Side into the batsman's legs.

OFF SIDE

The side farthest away from the batsman as he takes strike. For a right handed batsman it is the left side and for a left handed batsman the right side.

OFF SPIN

The name given to the type of bowling by a right handed bowler where the bowler uses his fingers to give spin to the ball as he makes his delivery. The Off Break is the stock delivery of an off spinner. When the same delivery is made by a left handed bowler it is said to be "unorthodox".

ON SIDE

The side nearest to the batsman as he takes strike. For a right handed batsman it is the right side and for a left handed batsman the left side.

OPENING PAIR

The "opening pair" are the first two batsmen in any side. They are expected to set the foundation for the batsmen after them to build on. The most prolific opening pair in Test Cricket for the West Indies were Gordon Greenidge and Desmond Haynes. Between 1978 and 1991 they accumulated 6482 runs at an average of 56.43 per innings.

OVERS

Overs are delivered alternately from each end by different bowlers. One over consists of six consecutive deliveries. In One Day Cricket the number of overs each bowler is allowed to bowl is determined by the rules of the specific competition. In Test Matches there is no limit.

OVER RATE

The number of overs bowled per hour. Fielding sides can be penalised for not completing the required number of overs on a given match day.

OVER THROWS

Where the fielder throws the ball to the wicket but it fails to be collected cleanly by the Wicket Keeper or fielder at the stumps and the batsmen run additional runs.

PADS

Leg pads are worn by batsmen and Wicket keepers

to protect them from the ankle area to mid-thigh. These were traditionally made of Canvas or Buckskin leather outers over cane and side wing padding. Modern pads are made from a synthetic material called PU. Arm, Thigh and Chest Pads are also used for protection.

PARTNERSHIP

The number of runs accumulated between two batsmen before one of them loses his wicket.

PENALTY RUNS

Penalty runs are treated as extras but they are recorded separately from the team official scores. Five Penalty Runs can be awarded for illegal fielding, time wasting by either team or the fielder damaging the pitch.

If the five penalty runs are awarded to the team batting they are recorded in the current innings of that team. If the five Penalty Runs are awarded to the fielding team, and they have not yet played an innings, then the penalty runs are added to their first innings.

Thus a side can start an innings with five or more runs already on the scoreboard.

PITCH

1. The area between the two bowling creases. The pitch should be 22 yards (20.12m) long by 10 feet (3.05m) wide with the center in line with the two middle stumps. It is bounded on either side by an imaginary line joining the centers of the two middle stumps, each parallel to it and 5 feet 1.52m) from it. See diagram at Creases page 15 .
2. The area where the ball bounces before reaching the batsman

POWER PLAYS

This is used in limited overs cricket and has replaced the former 15 over field restriction.

There is a mandatory field restriction within the first ten overs of the game when no more than two players can be outside the 30 yard circle and two in close catching positions inside the 30 yard circle. There is an additional ten over restriction which can be split into two sets of five overs to be taken at the fielding captains discretion. However if not used they automatically come into play at the latest available point in the innings. The two close catchers are not mandatory in the latter power plays.

RETIRE

An injured batsman may retire hurt from the field of play. When recovered the player may return to complete the innings at a later stage in the match.

REQUIRED RUN RATE

The rate at which the side batting second has to score to catch and overtake the opponents score.

This is particularly important in the short form of the game and can lead to nail biting excitement towards the closing stages of a match.

RUNS

Runs may be scored by

1. The batsmen running between the two wickets and grounding their bats in the opposite popping crease.
2. The batsman hitting the ball which travels along the ground to the boundary for four runs.
3. The batsman hitting the ball over the boundary in one motion for six runs.
4. Extras applied to a team's score for various infractions such as no balls bowled.

RUNNER

A runner is used when a batsman in the course of his innings is no longer able to run between the wickets due to an injury sustained during the course of the game.

RUN OUT

A batsman is run out :

1. When a Fielder with the ball in hand dislodges the bails before the batsman can gain his ground.

2. By a Fielder throwing the ball at the stumps and dislodging the bails before the batsman can gain his ground.

SCOREBOARD

Scoreboards are placed around the ground. The basic information given includes :

- The names of the batting side.
- Which batsmen are at the crease.
- How many runs each batsman has
- made.
- The number of overs.
- The score at the fall of the last wicket.
- The number of wickets which have fallen.
- Most modern grounds have large electronic scoreboards

As well as the required information as listed above they also show replays of match events such as run outs, catches and boundaries. They also show the fans in the stadium and sponsors advertisements.

A Traditinal Scoreboard

SCOREBOOK

The score book gives a detailed record of the game as it was played. It shows

1. The batting order;
2. Date, time, place
3. Name of competition;
4. Name of Umpires;
5. Weather conditions
6. How many runs each batsman made;
7. How the batsman got out;
8. Keeps a running total of the score;
9. Records extras and penalty runs;

10. Records the fall of wickets;
11. Bowling analysis summary.

SCORING

See Runs page 31 and Extras page 17.

SEAM

The ridge formed by the rows of stitching that join the two halves of the leather outer case of a cricket ball: the seam of a ball protrudes 1/4" above the rest of the surface, and this affects both the ball's trajectory through the air and the way that it moves after it pitches.

(See photo of ball with raised seams page 11)

SEAM BOWLER

A medium paced bowler who utilizes the seam of the ball to cause it to deviate from its line once it pitches by getting it to pitch on the seam rather than using the fingers to effect spin.

SESSION

One of the three official periods of play. In the long form of the game:

1. From Start of Play to Lunch;
2. From Lunch to Tea;
3. From Tea to the End of Play.

SHORT RUN

When a batsman running two or more runs fails to make his ground at one end.

The Umpire signals this and the scorer deducts the necessary run (runs).

SHORT PITCH

A type of bowling which invariably results in a Bouncer.

SIGHT SCREEN

These are large areas, usually white, found at both ends of the playing field in line with the wicket.

The purpose is to give the batsman a clear sighting of the bowlers arm and the ball as it is being bowled. When a white ball is used, the sightscreen is black.

SIX

The number of runs scored by one single hit of the ball over the boundary without touching the ground.

SLIPS

A close fielding position. First slip can usually be found on the Off Side about a foot behind the Wicketkeeper with the other slips a few feet apart.

SLIDER

A type of bowling action which is a combination of a leg break action with added side spin and back spin.

SQUARE LEG

A position square of the wicket to the left of the receiving batsman.

STUMPED

A batsman is out stumped if he is outside of his crease in an attempt to play the ball and the Wicket Keeper removes a bail with the ball in his gloved hand. The ball must pass the batsman before the Wicket Keeper can complete a stumping.

STUMPS

The three vertical wooden posts making up the wicket at either end of the pitch. They are set equal distances apart. Each stump is 28 inches (71.1cm)long with a circumference of no less than 1.38 inches (3.50cm). Also the call at the end of a day's play.

SUPER OVER

Primarily used in T20 Cricket where the match ends in a Tie. The super over consists of one over and two wickets for each team.

Runs scored in super overs do not count towards a player's statistical record.

TAIL ENDER

The name given to the last few batsmen in the team. These are usually made up of the specialist bowlers not usually known for their batting skills.

TEAM

In the professional game a cricket team is made up of eleven players and a substitute (twelfth man). It is usually composed of five specialist batsmen, five specialist bowlers and a Wicket Keeper.

TIMED OUT

When a batsman fails to take to the field within two minutes of the last batsman being given out the Umpire may send him back to the pavilion.

In this case he is said to have been "timed out".

THE TOSS

A coin is tossed by the home team Captain prior to the start of the game. The winning Captain chooses whether his team will bat or field first.

THIRD UMPIRE

The Third Umpire sits in the pavilion in front of a television monitor where he can review replays of the on field action.

The Umpire on the field may ask for assistance in cases of Run Outs, Stumpings, close line calls and disputed catches.

The television footage is reviewed and a decision is given by way of a red light to indicate out, or a green light to indicate not out.

TIE

Where both teams finish with the same aggregate score. Not to be confused with a Draw. There have been only two tied Test Matches both involving Australia. The first was during the 1960/61 tour between the West Indies and Australia at Brisbane and the second on the Australian tour to India at Madras in 1986. Both games went down to the last over and the last wicket on the last day.

TWELFTH MAN

A substitute player of the fielding side used where a

player has to leave the field of play for a valid reason.

UMPIRE

The name given to the match officials. There are usually two on field Umpires officiating at each match to enforce the laws of the game and ensure fair play. They are distinguished from the players by their black trousers and white coats or shirts. One Umpire stands at the bowlers wicket and the other at a position near Square Leg. The Umpire calls the start of play, the end of an over, indicates when Extras have been incurred.

Umpires alternate between square leg and behind the stumps for every other over.

The Umpire must be appealed to for a batsman to be given out. (See also Third Umpire page 37) .

Under the rules of cricket which came into effect on October 1st 2017 Umpires now have the power to award penalty points and/or send players off the field for unacceptable conduct.

UMPIRE DECISION REVIEW SYSTEM (DRS)

This is a system similar to the Challenge in Tennis. The Captain of the fielding side or the batsman can appeal to the Third Umpire to review a decision made by one of the on field Umpires. It is generally used in LBW and Run Out situations.

UMPIRE SIGNALS

(See Photographs pages 55-58)

WICKET

A set of wickets consists of three equally spaced wooden Stumps and two wooden Bails. Two sets are positioned on the Pitch 22yrd (20.12m) apart and opposite and parallel to each other. The total width of the three Stumps is 9" (22.86cm) and they should be positioned in a straight line and equally paced so as to prevent the ball passing between any two Stumps. The Bails are 4 3/8" (11.1cm) long and when in position should not protrude more than ½" above the top of the Stumps.

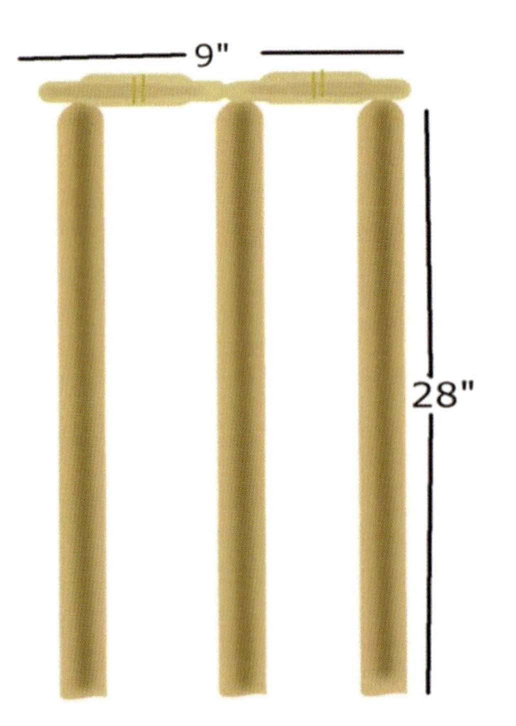

When a batsman is out he is said to have "lost his wicket".

WICKET KEEPER

This is a specialist fielding position. The Wicket Keeper stands behind the receiving batsman. He may be close up for the slow bowler or far back for the fast bowler. The major function of the Wicket Keeper is to stop deliveries that pass the batsman, saving byes and Leg Byes. The Wicket Keeper can affect dismissals by stumping and positioning himself to affect run outs.

WICKET MAIDEN

Where a bowler has completed an over without a run being scored but in which a wicket was taken.

WIDE

A delivery that is too high over or too wide of the Stumps for the batsman to make contact with the ball. The penalty is one run added to the batting sides score (an extra) and another delivery added to the over.

YORKER

A ball well pitched up so that it reaches the batsman's feet and is liable to pass under the bat.

A BRIEF HISTORY OF THE GAME

Mystery continues to surround the origins of the game of cricket. Some say it was brought to England from France, others that it arrived with the Normans and still others that it developed from shepherds playing in the field, throwing stones at each other and defending themselves with their staffs.

What can be verified is the fact that cricket was being played in England as far back as the 1550's. Court records indicate that there were a number of cases where persons were brought before the courts on misdemeanor charges related to playing cricket on a Sunday.

The game developed among the wealthy land owners who fielded the teams and their workers who were the players. The popularity of the game spread from country to town as the industrialised age brought about population movement and through the Public schools, like Eton and Harrow, where the land owners' sons were educated.

The game became such a popular spectator sport that in 1787 Thomas Lord leased a piece of land in Marylebone London and established a private cricket ground in order to keep the commoners out. The first match played at the newly formed Marylebone Cricket Club (MCC) was on May 31st 1787 when Middlesex played Essex. The club moved location several times finally coming to rest at the St. Johns Wood site we know today in 1814. The ground was named Lords in 1825 after the death of Thomas Lord and remains the bastion of English cricket to this day.

In 1788, the MCC published a set of Laws of Cricket, which contained the first complete set of rules of the game setting out the dimensions of the pitch and specifications for equipment. Other cricket clubs adopted the MCC's Laws and cricket became standardised for the first time. The MCC remains the custodian of the Laws of Cricket to the present day, updating them with new or changed rules from time to time. Individual leagues and governing bodies add their own playing regulations on top of these, amending the Laws to suit the differing needs of their situation. For example, in Switzerland the ball is always bowled from the same end, only the bowlers change.

The latest updates to the Lawes of Cricket by the MCC come into effect on October 1st 2017.

Although today it is not known for its cricket it was America which hosted the first international cricket game in 1844 when a club from Canada played at the St. George's Club in New York. During the 1870's the Philadelphia area was a stronghold for cricket. Cricket remained a popular sport with regular games played between teams from Canada and England. However the American Civil War put a temporary end to these matches which allowed the fledgling sport of baseball to emerge as the favoured team sport of Americans.

The game as we know it today stems from the introduction of the legislation of over arm bowling in 1864. Prior to that the ball was lobbed under arm. By that date First Class cricket was being played in England, Australia, New Zealand, the West Indies and South Africa. This was the era of one of the most famous cricketers of the time William Gilbert (WG) Grace.

The popularity of the game outside of England can be attributed to British Colonisation. Wherever the British Army had a Garrison there was provision made for a cricket pitch, hence the popularity of the game in countries as diverse as Australia and Zimbabwe.

Although cricket may appear to be a male dominated sport it is also played professionally by women. The same rules and regulations apply and like the male game it is played locally, regionally and internationally. Claire Taylor of England became the first female to feature on a Hall of Fame board at Lords ground when on August 14th 2006 she scored 156 runs in a match played there against India. It was the top One Day International score at that ground eclipsing the record of 138 set in 1979 by West Indian batsman Sir Vivian Richards.

SPECTATOR ETIQUETTE

Attendance at a First Class cricket match is a day out to be savoured and enjoyed. Like Boy Scouts you should be prepared. In hot climates make sure that you walk with your sun screen. Even in the covered stands facing the west, what may be cool shade in the morning can become hot in the afternoon as the day draws towards sunset. In cooler climes be prepared to keep warm and always prepare for a down pour of rain. You could be in the midst of the severest drought but as soon as the words "cricket match" are uttered down comes the rain.

Those who arrive early for the game will have the opportunity to see the teams warming up on the field and going through their drills. Where net facilities are available you could get a chance to see the players up close and may be able to get an autograph or two.

The majority of cricket grounds today have covered stands and hospitality suites as well as "mounds" or grassy areas that are uncovered for spectators to view the game. A good position would be one where you can see the line of the ball as the bowler bowls to the batsman.

If you listen to the commentary on the radio while watching the match have your own headphones so that you do not disturb the other spectators. Once the game has started and you must leave and subsequently return to your seat wait until the end of the over or while the bowler is making his way back to his mark.

Cricket crowds can be as boisterous as any other sport's fans, however the vast majority of fans will show respect and admiration for opponents and their performances. Significant achievements on the field by players of the home team or the visitors such as a batsman making a hundred runs or an athletic catch in the field, are always greeted with warm applause and standing ovations where warranted.

VARIATIONS OF THE GAME

TEST CRICKET

The word "Test" in relation to cricket was first used in 1861-62 when an English team toured Australia. It was then considered to be a "test" of strength between the participating sides. Those matches may not be considered Test Match quality by today's standards but they set the stage for the format as we know it today, a series of matches between the top cricketing nations.

Features of Test Matches are:

- The players wear white or off white clothing.
- Five days are allotted for a Test Match.
- Each team has a cap that is presented to a player when he makes his debut for his national side.
- The ball played with is red (or pink for Day/Night Tests).
- The sight screens are white.
- A bowler can bowl as many overs as his captain asks of him.
- The captain can place his fielders in any position on the field.
- There are two innings per side.
- There are three possible outcomes to the match; win, draw or tie.
- The fielding side can change the ball after every 80 overs.

- At least 90 overs are expected to be bowled per day.

Test Matches are usually played in one territory as a series between two nations with each match scheduled for five days. There are usually three to five tests in each tour and often there is a particular trophy that is being played for. Two of the better known series are "The Ashes" played for between England and Australia and the "Frank Worrell Trophy" played for between the West Indies and Australia.

On June 15th 1909, representatives of England, Australia and South Africa met at Lords and established the Imperial Cricket Conference (ICC). The ICC became the International Cricket Council which is currently the governing body for International Cricket.

There are currently twelve nations that are recognised as having Test playing status. These are England, Australia, South Africa, The West Indies, New Zealand, India, Pakistan, Sri Lanka, Bangladesh, Zimbabwe, Ireland and Afghanistan.

The Test Match is considered by the purist to be the highest form of the game, calling for long hours of concentration by batsmen and highlighting the tactical decisions of the fielding captain.

FIRST CLASS CRICKET

The highest form of the game played locally within the test playing nations and from which the international teams are usually chosen.

English county cricket used to be the nursery from which many test players from all the test playing nations emerged.

The game is played to the same format as Test Cricket but is usually of three or four days in duration. Each territory or region have their own tournaments which are played during the cricket season. There are also one off games such as the warm up matches played before the start of a Test series or special invitational matches.

ONE DAY CRICKET

There are a number of distinctions between the One Day version of the game and Test Cricket:

- Players wear coloured clothing.
- Overs are limited.
- There is only one innings per side.
- The white ball is used.
- The sight screens are black.
- There are field placement and bowling restrictions.
- There are stricter rules on wide balls and short deliveries.
- There may be a day/night format to the game where the first innings is played starting in daylight and the second innings under artificial lighting.

The first match in the One Day format was played in England in 1963 when Leicestershire beat Lancashire at Manchester. Since that time there have been a number of

One Day tournaments played locally, regionally and internationally.

The first One Day International (ODI) was played between England and Australia in Melbourne during the 1971 tour and it has become part of the itinerary of all touring sides since then.

The International Cricket Council's World Cup is a knock out One Day tournament played every four years between the Test playing nations and qualifying associate nations. It consists of a series of round robin games, then proceeds to a knockout format. The first tournament was played in England in 1975 and won by the West Indies.

TWENTY/20 CRICKET (T-20)

Twenty/20 Cricket is the latest evolution in the game of cricket. As the name suggests it is a twenty over a side game which is usually completed within three hours, thereby always providing a result. It has a similar duration in time to a football or basketball game making it very marketable to television audiences.

There are many similarities to One Day Cricket, in that there are a limited number of overs, there are restrictions on field placings, the players wear coloured clothing and play with a white ball.

Twenty/20 Cricket was first played in England amongst the county teams in 2003. One of the advantages of this version of the game is that it can act as a showcase for the talents of young players without too much pressure to perform being placed on them.

The first tournament sporting a million dollar prize was sponsored by entrepreneur Allen Stanford and played at the Stanford Cricket Ground on the island of Antigua. It was the first Twenty/20 tournament played in the West Indies and was contested by 19 teams, the eventual winner being Guyana. This was the first cricket tournament which sported such high prize money for the winning team and the governing cricket body.

Since that time T20 cricket, as it has become known, has seen the growth of a number of high prize money tournaments. In 2008 the Indian Premier League came into being. In 2011 the Big Bash in Australia and in 2013 the West Indian version was revived with the formation of the Caribbean Premier League. These tournaments consists of a series of round-robin group matches, then proceeds to a knockout format.

Each tournament includes professional players from outside their regions as well as young up and coming players.

The T20 Championships have become very popular with fans. These matches are Fun and Fast with Carnival like, family outing type, atmospheres. However this popularity has not totally eclipsed the Test Match as exemplified by the recent addition of Ireland and Afghanistan to Test playing status. The Test Match will continue to be the ultimate "test" of a player's ability.

FIELDING POSITION

For a Right Handed Batsman

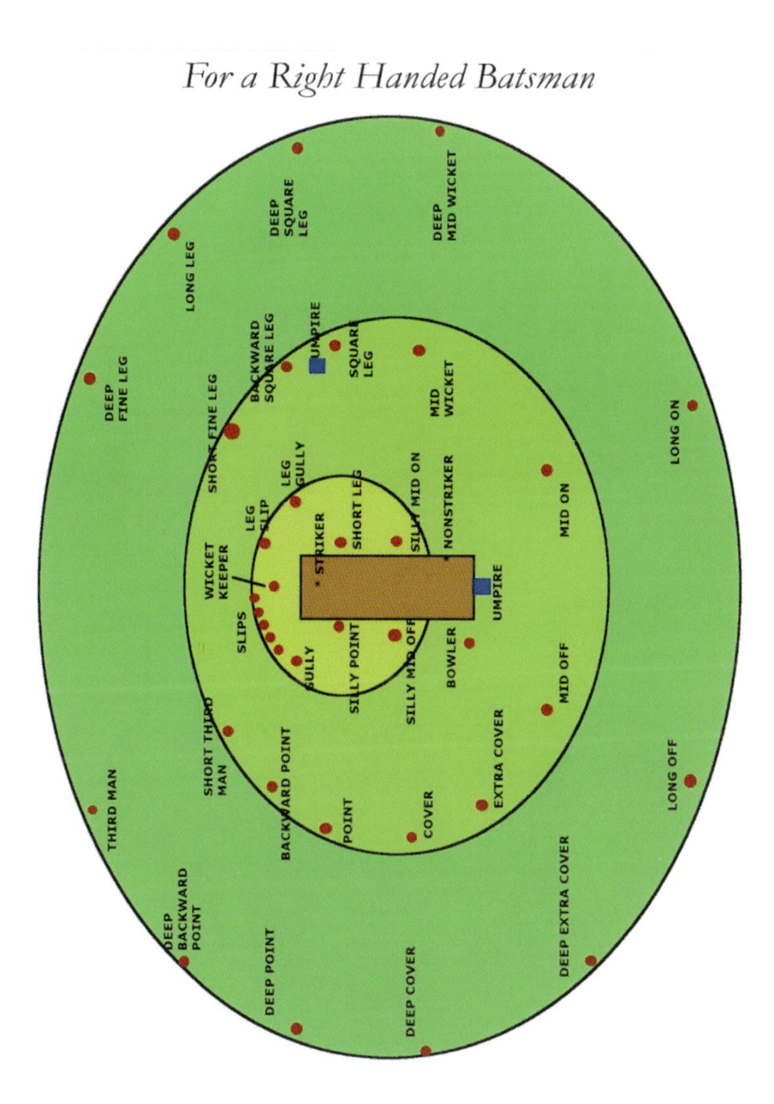

CRICKET EQUIPMENT

UMPIRE SIGNALS

SIX RUNS

The umpire raises both hands towards the sky

BYE

The umpire raises one hand high above his body

FOUR RUNS

The umpire waves his hand from side to side finishing with his hand across his chest

DEAD BALL

The umpire crosses his wrists in the area of his knees

WIDE

The umpire holds both hands outstretched

SHORT RUNS

The umpire touches one shoulder with the hand of the same shoulder

NO BALL

The umpire stretches out one hand at shoulder height

LEG BYES

The umpire touches his raised knee with his hand

OUT

The umpire raise one finger

NEW BALL

The umpire shows the new ball to the scorers

LAST HOUR

The umpire taps his watch to indicate the start of the last hour of play

RESCIND LAST SIGNAL

The umpire crosses his hands across his chest to indicate a mistake in the last decision

PENALTY POINTS FIELDING SIDE

The umpire brings one hand across his chest and rests it on the opposite shoulder

PENALTY POINTS BATTING SIDE

The umpire brings one hand across his chest and taps the opposite shoulder

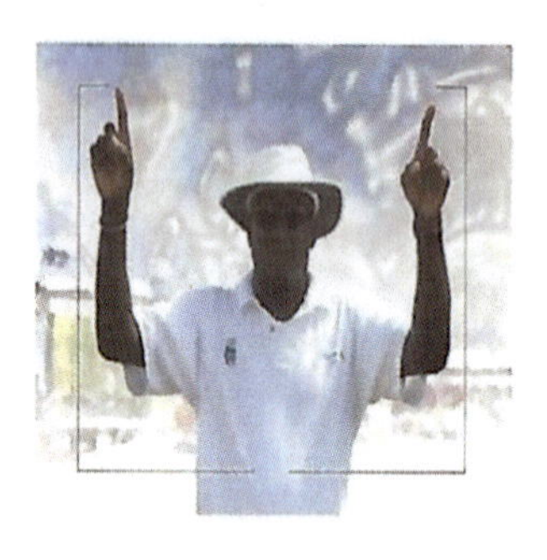

TELEVISION REPLAY

The umpire makes the sign of a square in the air using both hands

POWERPLAY

The umpire makes a circle in the air

GUIDE TO SCORING CRICKET

Cricket matches need scorers to record runs scored, wickets taken and overs bowled.

The purpose of this Guide is to give guidance to those who are new to scoring and players who score only part of an innings

THE BATTING SECTION OF THE SCORING RECORD

- You should have received a team list, hopefully with the batting order identified.
- Record the name of the batsman in pencil or as the innings progresses - captains often change the batting order!
- Indicate the captain with an asterisk (*) and the wicket keeper with a dagger symbol (†).
- When a batsman is out, draw diagonal lines // in the 'Runs Scored' section after all entries for that batsman to show that the innings is completed.
- Record the method of dismissal in the "**how out**" column.
- Write the bowler's name in the "**bowler**" column ***only*** if the bowler gets credit for the dismissal.
- When a batsman's innings is completed record his total score.

CUMULATIVE SCORE

- Use one stroke to cross off each incident of runs scored.
- When more than one run is scored and the total is taken onto the next row of the cumulator this should be indicated as shown below.

Cumulative Run Tally									
	1	2	3	4	5	6	7	8	9
10	11	12	13	14	15	16	17	18	19

END OF OVER SCORE

- At the end of each over enter the total score, number of wickets fallen and bowler number.

THE BOWLING SECTION OF THE SCORING RECORD

The over

- Always record the balls in the over in the same sequence in the overs box.
- An over containing Wide or No balls, show balls ***7 & 8*** as highlighted.

1	2	3
7	***8***	
4	5	6

1	***7***	4
2	***8***	5
3		6

- All balls bowled must be entered.
- If the umpire gives a 7 ball over record a 7 ball over.
- If there are only 5 deliveries in the over that is all you should record.
- A Maiden over is a complete over by a single bowler in which there is no score against that
- bowler. The dots should be joined together to form an "**M**".
- A Maiden over *cannot* contain a Wide ball or a No ball.
- An accidental 5 or 7 ball over is a completed over when counting up the number of overs
- bowled. As a completed over, it can be a Maiden over.
- A part over for any other reason can never be a Maiden over.
- If a wicket falls that is credited to the bowler enter a "w" for that delivery.
- If a wicket credited to the bowler falls in a Maiden over it becomes a 'wicket maiden'. Join the dots and "w" together to form a "**W**".
- Numerals are used **only** for runs made when the ball has been struck by the bat.

BYES AND LEG BYES

- Can be entered as a dot but it is better to use a symbol.

Byes	Triangle, point upwards	Δ
Leg byes	Triangle, point down	∇

- Runs made as byes or leg byes are recorded in the appropriate line of fielding extras.

WIDES AND NO BALLS

- Under MCC Laws of Cricket a one run penalty is awarded for a No ball or a Wide in addition to any other runs made.
- All Wide balls and No balls count against the bowler in the bowling analysis.
- An over containing a Wide ball or a No ball cannot be a maiden over.
- A Wide or a No ball is not a fair delivery and does not count as a ball in the over.
- If a wicket falls when a Wide ball or No ball has been bowled and there are no other runs, record the 1 run penalty *before* entering the score at the fall of the wicket.

SUMMARISE THE BOWLING

- Complete the total number of overs, maidens, runs and wickets for each bowler at the end of the innings.
- If an over is incomplete each *fair* delivery in the part over is expressed as 0.1 ball.
- Calculate and record the number of no ball and wide deliveries, the total number of balls bowled and the average for each bowler.
- Total these figures to provide a summary of balls, overs, maidens, runs and wickets for the entire innings.

RECORDING THE SCORE FROM A NO BALL DELIVERY

BALL NOT HIT BY STRIKER	SCORED AS	RECORDED AS
Batsmen do not run	1 No Ball EXTRA	○
Batsmen run 1, 2 or 3	2, 3 or 4 No Ball EXTRAS	⊙ ⊙ ⊙
Batsmen run 4 or ball crosses the boundary	5 No Ball EXTRAS	⊙

BALL HIT BY STRIKER	SCORED AS	RECORDED AS
Batsmen do not run	1 No Ball EXTRA	○
Batsmen run 1, 2 or 3	1,2 or 3 to STRIKER & 1 No Ball EXTRA	① ② ③
Boundary 4 or 6 signalled	4 or 6 to STRIKER & 1 No ball EXTRA	④ ⑥

RECORDING THE SCORE FROM A WIDE DELIVERY (A WIDE BALL CANNOT BE HIT)

	SCORED AS	RECORDED AS
Batsmen do not run	1 Wide EXTRA	+
Batsmen run 1, 2 or 3	2, 3 or 4 Wide EXTRAS	+ + +
Boundary signalled	5 Wide EXTRAS	+
Batsman out Stumped or Hit Wicket (wicket credited to bowler)	1 Wide Extra	+

SCORING SHEETS

MATCH VENUE..DATE..

..............INNINGS..VERSUS...

	BATSMAN		HOW OUT	BOWLERS	TOTAL RUNS
1					
2					
3					
4					
5					
6					
7					
8					
9					
10					
11					

BYES...............................LEG BYES.......................WIDE BALLS...............................NO BALLS.......................................

1 FOR	2 FOR	3 FOR	4 FOR	5 FOR	6 FOR	7 FOR	8 FOR	9 FOR	10 FOR	TOTAL

BOWLING ANALYSIS

BOWLER	OVERS	MAIDENS	RUNS	WICKETS

MATCH VENUE..DATE..

.............INNINGS..VERSUS..

	BATSMAN		HOW OUT	BOWLERS	TOTAL RUNS
1					
2					
3					
4					
5					
6					
7					
8					
9					
10					
11					

BYES.................................LEG BYES.......................WIDE BALLS...............................NO BALLS.......................................

1 FOR	2 FOR	3 FOR	4 FOR	5 FOR	6 FOR	7 FOR	8 FOR	9 FOR	10 FOR	TOTAL

BOWLING ANALYSIS

BOWLER	OVERS	MAIDENS	RUNS	WICKETS

MATCH VENUE..DATE..

..............INNINGS..VERSUS..

	BATSMAN		HOW OUT	BOWLERS	TOTAL RUNS
1					
2					
3					
4					
5					
6					
7					
8					
9					
10					
11					

BYES.................................LEG BYES......................WIDE BALLS.............................NO BALLS..

1 FOR	2 FOR	3 FOR	4 FOR	5 FOR	6 FOR	7 FOR	8 FOR	9 FOR	10 FOR	TOTAL

BOWLING ANALYSIS

BOWLER	OVERS	MAIDENS	RUNS	WICKETS

MATCH VENUE...DATE..

.............INNINGS...VERSUS..

	BATSMAN		HOW OUT	BOWLERS	TOTAL RUNS
1					
2					
3					
4					
5					
6					
7					
8					
9					
10					
11					

BYES..............................LEG BYES......................WIDE BALLS...........................NO BALLS.....................................

1 FOR	2 FOR	3 FOR	4 FOR	5 FOR	6 FOR	7 FOR	8 FOR	9 FOR	10 FOR	TOTAL

BOWLING ANALYSIS

BOWLER	OVERS	MAIDENS	RUNS	WICKETS

BIBLIOGRAPHY

Arnold, Peter & Wynne-Thomas, Peter: The Ultimate Encyclopedia of Cricket (Carlton Press 2004)

Morrison, Ian: Cricket - Play the Game (Blandford 1993)

Rundel, Michael: The Dictionary of Cricket (Oxford University Press 1996)

Smith, Tom: Tom Smith's New Cricket Umpiring and Scoring (Winfield & Nicolson 2004)

OTHER RESOURCES

BBC Sport - Cricket

DM's Explanation of Cricket

Wikipedia - The Free Encyclopedia

If you're interested in the updated Laws of Cricket as at October 1st 2017 they can be found on our Cricket page at Bluepalmpublications.com.

We hope that you found this book useful and that it contributes to your understanding and enjoyment of the game of Cricket.

We respect your feedback and would appreciate it if you can leave a review on Amazon to inform future Cricket fans.

This book is also available as an eBook and a downloadable pdf from the cricket page at our publishing site

bluepalmpublications.com

and see what else Miriam has in store at

https://mimsbooksandthings.blogspot.com/

ABOUT THE AUTHOR

Miriam Rice-Walcott is a native of Barbados currently residing in Guyana.

Miriam wrote her first cricket book as a handy pocket guide that could be used for reference while watching or listening to a cricket match, for the novice spectator of the game. This book continues in the same vein with the added benefit of being available as an eBook and thereby accessible on any smart phone or other electronic device.

Miriam is also the author and independent publisher of a number of bestselling colouring books for adults with Blue Palm Publications.

You can connect with her on:
Facebook:
https://www.facebook.com/bluepalmadultcolouringbooks/
Twitter: https://twitter.com/bluepalmpublic2
Pinterest: https://pinterest.com/mlwenterprises
Instagram:
https://www.instagram.com/bluepalmpublications
www.mimsbooksandthings.blogspot.com
www.bluepalmpublications.com

From Blue Palm Publications
Sign up for our First Serve List
on our Cricket page
at
www.bluepalmpublications.com

The Cricketers Journal

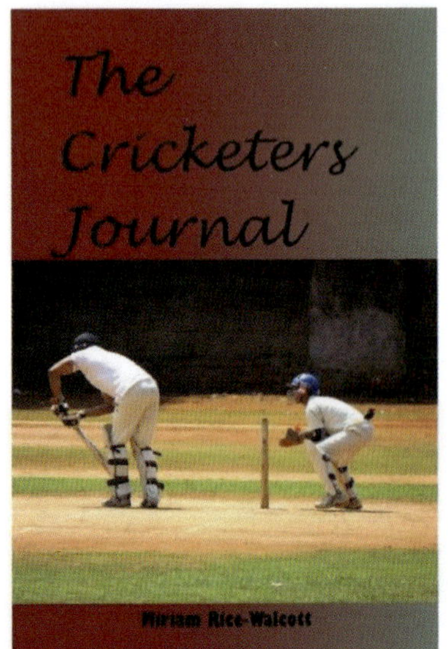

Whether Cricketer or Spectator this Journal will come in handy to

- Record your favourite sporting moments
- Keep records of your favourite teams
- Record personal goals
- And much much more

This Journal makes an ideal gift especially for the budding Cricketers in your life

Printed in Great Britain
by Amazon